KE
RAM

Ten Country Walks around the Garden of England

Roy Plascott

With Historical Notes

COUNTRYSIDE BOOKS
NEWBURY, BERKSHIRE

First Published 1987
Reprinted 1990, 1991
Revised and updated 1994

COUNTRYSIDE BOOKS
3 Catherine Road
Newbury, Berkshire
ISBN 0 905392 76 0

Cover Photograph of Boughton Aluph by Tim Sharman
Sketch Maps by Arthur Prosser
Produced through MRM Associates Ltd, Reading
Printed in England by J. W. Arrowsmith Ltd., Bristol

Contents

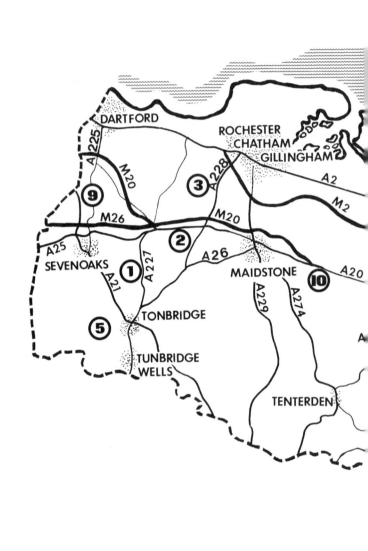

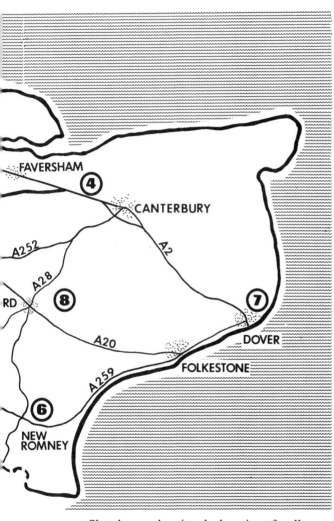

Sketch map showing the location of walks.

Publisher's Introduction

The walks in this book have been chosen because they offer a good variety of the county's diversity of delightful scenery. This ranges from downland to marshes, rivers and coastline, forests and orchards, farmland, stately homes and castles. The County has four long distance footpaths: the North Downs Way, the Saxon Shore Way, the Weald Way and the Greensand Way. Parts of these feature in several of the walks. Other routes include the Darent Valley Path and the Eden Valley Walk.

All the walks are circular and their starting points have space for car parking. Public transport is shown where it is available. For those who like to break their walk for refreshment the names of good pubs and places serving tea along or near the routes are mentioned.

The historical notes are designed to provide basic information about the places of interest along the route, and will be found at the end of each chapter.

The sketch map that accompanies each walk is designed to guide walkers to the starting point and give a simple but accurate idea of the route to be taken. For those who like the benefit of detailed maps the relevant Ordnance Survey series sheet 1:50 000 series is recommended.

The walks are all along public footpaths and highways, but do bear in mind that deviation orders may be made from time to time. Please also remember the Country Code and make sure gates are not left open nor any farm animals disturbed.

The Footpaths Department of Kent County Council has co-operated to make the route descriptions as foolproof as possible. But the public footpaths enjoyed by walkers are not signposted, waymarked and cleared by magic. The local authorities who have an obligation to maintain footpaths rely heavily on volunteers to help with the work. Should you have enjoyed these walks so much that you feel inspired to join in this valuable work, please contact your local foot-path group or Ramblers' Association.

No special equipment is needed to enjoy the countryside on foot, but do wear a stout pair of shoes and remember that at least one muddy patch is likely even on the sunniest day.

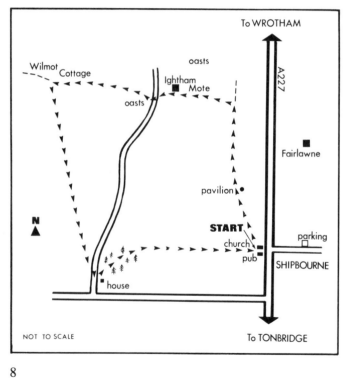

To WROTHAM

oasts

Wilmot Cottage

A227

Ightham Mote

oasts

oasts

Fairlawne

pavilion

START

N

parking

church

pub

SHIPBOURNE

house

NOT TO SCALE

To TONBRIDGE

8

Shipbourne
and Ightham Mote

Introduction: Many Kent ramblers will maintain that this area is one of the best parts in which to walk in the whole county. One stretch of this particular excursion follows the Greensand Way, the latest long-distance path for walkers in West Kent. You are able to have a brief taste of this footpath and by doubling back over different terrain you have an outing well within the capability of the average family, providing some spectacular views. As an added bonus the walk provides an intimate look at Ightham Mote, a fourteenth century manor house and a glimpse of Fairlawne, a later mansion with Royal connections.

Distance: The walk is about 5 miles, taking the leisurely walker about 2½ hours.

Refreshments: There is a public house called The Chaser at the beginning of the walk which provides meals seven days a week.

How to get there: The start is at Shipbourne (pronounced Shibbun) a village on the A227 between Wrotham and Tonbridge. Park by the common road - Upper Green Road - opposite the church.

The walk: The walk begins at Shipbourne's tall, grey Victorian church on the other side of the main road. Through the lychgate, use the path to the right of the church to find a gate in the old grey wall at the back of the churchyard. No fewer than three footpaths radiate from this point. Take the path on the extreme right.

The view ahead is handsome - over fields and woodland and beyond the Greensand Ridge which you will in due course climb. From the churchyard follow the field boundary to the right. It veers left and right by a large modern house.

Go over the stile in the corner of the field. A sign indicates that you are now on the Greensand Way. Half right from the stile, there is an established path across an open field towards a line of trees about 100 yards away.

At the trees cross a stile and then follow the hedge and fence on the right, noticing a cloak of conifers on the low hill to the left. The boundary bends left and right in the corner of the field. There is a cricket pavilion over the hedge on the right. Cross a concrete bridge. Ignore two farm gates on the left and follow the boundary as it bends to the left.

Follow the field edge and soon you will spot Fairlawne, the red and white mansion. Continue to a stile and some double gates. After about 150 yards go through a wooden gate and continue. On the left are some typical Kent oasthouses, with characteristic conical roofs, happily well preserved. After about 100 yards go over a stile on the left by a gate. Walk along a bridleway for a few hundred yards, passing a National Trust sign for Ightham Mote. Ahead you see the Greensand Ridge waiting to be climbed.

The track ends among trees in which you find, unexpectedly tucked away, beautiful Ightham Mote. The right of way goes alongside the moat and house with a pond on the left, populated by many birds. You may hear the strident cry of the resident peacock and if lucky see him spread his tail feathers. Walk along the drive to a lane.

Here you go right for a dozen yards to turn left into a farmyard. Ahead is a pair of oasts. Your way runs to the right just short of them and continues as a narrow flinty track upwards. This is the beginning of the climb. It pays to stop and look behind you now and then, the better to appreciate the fine views.

Keep to the main track and soon you will reach a stile by a metal gate leading into a wooded area. The track goes downhill, but not for long and soon you are on the up again. Look out, particularly on the right for large hunks of rock which are reminders of the Greensand Ridge. On the left you begin to see the fine views towards Tonbridge and Sevenoaks.

Presently you will see Wilmot Cottage on the right and here you leave the Greensand Way by taking a stile to the left. This is worth a pause here, for the views are simply marvellous. Half left you will see the grey stump of Shipbourne Church which is of course your final objective.

Walk directly down the steep pasture to an easily seen stile. Follow the right boundary of the next field. Continue ahead over a well-marked path through a field to a plank over a ditch. Cross the next field to a stile to a lane.

Walk right for about 10 yards and use the stile on the left short of a house into a conifer plantation. You follow a wide, grassy ride between trees. At a fork veer left. The ground can be spongy here after rain. Ignore side paths which are marked 'private'. On reaching a junction of five paths down a gentle slope, take the second on the right so that you have a tree hedge with a field beyond on the left and conifers on the right.

11

A stile at the end leads to a field and you will easily see the path as it runs through a gap in a hedge to the back of the church where the walk began.

Shipbourne and Ightham Mote — Historical Notes

Ightham Mote: One of the most important medieval manor houses in Britain, made more interesting in that it has been continuously lived in since it was built in 1340. It was given to the National Trust in 1985 by the wealthy American Charles Henry Robinson. The original Great Hall is still there and important additions were made, particularly a fine staircase in Jacobean times. The Tudor chapel was built between 1521 and 1529 and entirely rebuilt in 1890-1891 by the then owner Thomas Colyer-Fergusson using as much of the original material as possible. The walls of the crypt below are four feet thick. The first owner was Sir Thomas Cawne who lived there from 1340 until his death in 1374. He was responsible for the moat and the building of the Great Hall, the old chapel and crypt and the gate house. A later occupant was Dorothy Selby, who some historians say, tipped off the King and Parliament about the Guy Fawkes' Gunpowder Plot in 1605. The house is open to the public from 11am to 5pm on Mondays, Wednesdays, Thursdays, Fridays and Sundays.

The Greensand Ridge: This is a geological feature roughly parallel with the North Downs. After the great Wealden lake in the south-east of England became salt water after an up-heaval of the earth's surface millions of years ago, sandstone began to be formed. This rock has been used for buildings from Roman times. Part of London's ancient walls were made from this sandstone.

Wilmot Cottage: Reputed to have been an alehouse on an old pack-horse way between Kent and London, taking in places like Ightham Mote and Knole, Sevenoaks.

The Chaser: This public house, formerly the New Inn, was given its name 25 years ago by the landlord because of the racing stables at the nearby mansion, Fairlawne and as a pun on the style of drink. The inn sign contains a humorous picture of a rider jumping a fence.

Fairlawne: A handsome red-brick mansion with a belfry built in the early eighteenth century with additions in the first half of the nineteenth. Its more recent claim to fame was that it had in its grounds racing stables run by the Cazelet family. Among horses trained there were those owned by the Queen Mother. After Peter Cazelet died in 1973, the estate was sold to pay the death duties.

Shipbourne Church: Built on the site of an earlier church, the present St Giles Church was constructed in late Victorian times. The body of Sir Harry Vane, the seventeenth century statesman and close friend of Oliver Cromwell, was interred here after he was beheaded in 1662. This followed the Restoration of Charles II two years earlier and was despite the fact that Vane had not been directly involved in the execution of Charles I during the Civil Wars.

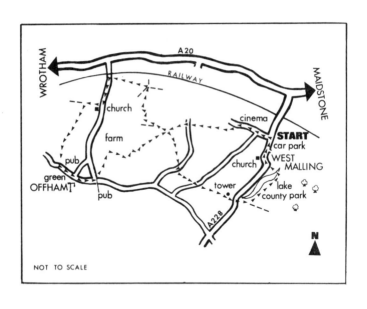

WROTHAM

A 20

RAILWAY

MAIDSTONE

church

farm

cinema

START
car park

pub

church

WEST
MALLING

green
OFFHAM

pub

tower

lake
county park

A228

N

NOT TO SCALE

West Malling and Offham

Introduction: The North Downs, that ridge of high ground which runs through Kent, forms an impressive backdrop throughout this walk. It begins at West Malling, a delightful community round a wide, ancient main street which cannot make up its mind whether it should be described as a village or a town. There are Georgian houses and everywhere grey stones are witness to much earlier occupation. The eleventh century square St Leonard's Tower is a feature to the south of West Malling and is passed on the walk. The walk also takes in the village of Offham which on its spacious green has a quintain - a medieval jousting device.

Distance: This walk is 4½ miles on mostly level ground and can be accomplished in about 2 hours.

Refreshments: West Malling is well endowed with restaurants, cafes and pubs. Half way round the route, at Offham, there are two pubs, the King's Arms and the Red Lion, not far from the village green.

How to get there: West Malling is just off the A20 between Maidstone and Wrotham. It is served by a railway station. There is a large public car park in the High Street.

The walk: From the car park walk right down the wide main
street and cross over to go down West Street, a narrow road
with a few shops under a sort of verandah. Do not go down
Offham Road to the left, but continue along the road
beside playing fields and modern houses. As the road
curves right look out for a 'no fouling' sign and go up the
alley by it to a road. An alleyway runs by a red brick wall
to the right which takes you to another street of houses.
Cross over to go down another alley opposite which takes
you past a playing field into open country.

For the first time on the walk, you see how the North
Downs dominate the landscape. Reaching a lane, go
over the stile in the hedge opposite and follow the right
boundary. At the corner go left to follow the hedge on the
right.

A gap in the hedge at the end, marked by a post, takes
you into a field where you turn right. In the middle
distance you will see some oasts with conical roofs. Keep
to the right edge of the field edged by trees and at the end
veer a little to the right to follow a track along the left-
hand edge of the field and then bear right at a line of trees.
Bend left, then right again. At the end of the trees, where
there are splendid views of the Downs, turn left and
follow a path with wire fencing on the right. Ignore an
opening into a field beyond the trees. Follow the path
down to the lane and bear left. Just before Offham's tiny
church, take the concrete farm road to the right. It is, of
course, a good idea to deviate for a few yards to see the
church properly. There is a handsome thatched, black
weatherboarded barn just beyond it.

The concrete farm road takes you through a complex of
buildings. Immediately beyond the house on the left,
follow the path round to the left so that you have the
Downs over your shoulder. The path plunges into wood-

land, where you go left at a junction of paths for a residential road.

Walk ahead to the main road through Offham. A left turn takes you by the King's Arms pub and the green with the celebrated quintain. Continue along the village street - Teston (pronounced Teeson) Road.

At the Red Lion pub on the left, take the marked footpath on its right side with a grey stone wall initially on the right. The stile at the end takes you into an open field where you follow a path to the right. After a few yards bear left and head towards a farm and oasthouse. Within about 50 yards of a farm take the path to the right. You will see a line of poplars in the distance. At a hedge, walk left and after a few yards turn right in the field corner into the next field. Walk along the field edge, passing several pine trees. Look for a waymarker post, with a copse on the right. Within a couple of yards you will find a footpath into the small woodland.

At an open field on the other side, go half left on an easily seen path as there is smooth grass through rough ground, meeting a hedge coming up from the left. A stile takes you into a lane on the left. Walk up the lane with pine trees on the left to find a track on the left just short of a house. It leads to a lane where you cross over slightly left for a roughish road.

At the end is the ancient monument, St Leonard's Tower and the main road. Cross this into Manor Country Park passing white-fronted cottages on the right.

In the park, go over the driveway and take the path on the right side of the long, narrow lake. On the rising ground beyond the lake you will see Douce's Manor, now a training centre for an insurance company. Almost at the end of the lake, which has swans and other water birds, go over a little bridge, up steps to find a gate to the main road.

A right turn takes you back to the car park, passing on the

17

way, on the left, the needle-like steepled parish church and the old village pump.

West Malling - Historical Notes

West Malling: The Norman conquest brought status to the hitherto unimportant community with the founding of an abbey for Benedictine nuns by Bishop Gundulf of Rochester in the eleventh century. The medieval gatehouse survives but the modern buildings - St Mary's Abbey - in Swan Street are nowadays occupied by an enclosed order of Anglican Benedictine nuns.

St Leonard's Tower: Gundulf was also responsible for the fortified keep, the remains of which are today an English Heritage Ancient Monument, built mainly of flint and ragstone.

Village Pump: Dating from 1850, the pump was restored by the Royal Engineers to mark the Silver Jubilee of Queen Elizabeth's reign.

West Malling Parish Church: The tower and part of the chancel of St Mary's built in Norman times survive. The nave had to be re-built in the eighteenth century because there were so many burials within the church that the foundations were weakened and the whole structure became dangerous. One vicar, Samuel French, who was a Puritan, was sent to prison for six months for his non-conformity after the Restoration of The Monarchy in 1660.

Offham Church: The tiny church remains much as it was in the fourteenth century, although parts of the walls date back to the eleventh century. St John the Evangelist features in a fifteenth century glass window in the upper part of the south-west window.

Offham's Quintain: In medieval times young men on horseback had to ride fast and strike the flat end of an arm swivelling on a post with a lance. The trick was to ride out of the way before a bag of sand on the other end of the arm hit them in the back of the neck.

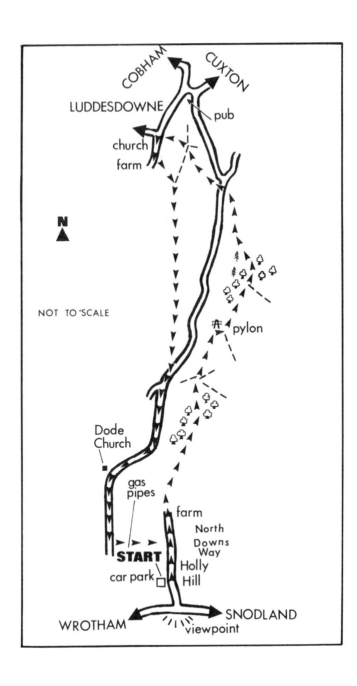

Holly Hill and Luddesdowne

Introduction: This pretty walk in one of the unspoilt parts of well-populated north Kent is enjoyed by ramblers today because it was reprieved from use as an army training ground due to the efforts of local people and conservationists. Curiously, while the valley between Luddesdowne and Holly Hill is sparsely populated today, the village of Dode once flourished there. Its population was wiped out by the Black Death in the fourteenth century, and all that remains is a tiny church which is a feature of this walk.

Distance: This 4½ mile excursion is easy for the average walker, and will take about 2 hours.

Refreshments: The Golden Lion at Luddesdowne serves food. A cottage just off the route at one point serves soft drinks and sweets.

How to get there: The starting point is a public car park serving Holly Hill, one of the North Downs prime viewing points. At the Wrotham roundabout on the A20 take the Gravesend A227 road. Just past the Vigo Inn on the right, take the road to the right signposted to Trosley Country Park. This is not the same place as Holly Hill. You proceed along the road for about two miles, ignoring side turnings.

Where the road narrows considerably and is overhung with trees, look out for a no-through-lane on the left. (The best viewpoint over the North Downs is on the right and you might like to visit it later). Along the no-through-road on the left you will find a car park next to a cottage. The car park gates close at dusk.

The Walk: Leaving the car park, walk left down the country lane which is in fact part of the North Downs Way. Beyond Holly Hill Farm with its castellated features, the lane becomes a rough path. Continue ahead on the level, ignoring a path downhill to the left. The North Downs Way runs along a wooded ridge at this point. Because it is also used by horse-riders, the earth is churned up in places, but you will usually find little 'by-passes' in the woodland on either side which walkers have made in the worst places.

In due course you come to a junction of paths where a short distance down a path to the left you will find a place where you may buy soft drinks and confectionery. However, your walk continues on the level straight ahead and leaves the North Downs Way which goes off across a field to the right.

The terrain is similar to that which you have just come through. When a power line pylon looms in front of you, the path veers to the right. Where it joins a path coming in from the right, go left. The walk runs between trees; further on look out for a dilapidated gate on the right. Here on warm summer nights you can hear nightingales sing.

You do not go into this area, but instead go on the path through the trees ahead. Follow the chalky path downhill to a lane. Cross over to take a path indicated by a stone to a group of trees. In the middle distance ahead you will see the tower of Luddesdowne Church for which you are aiming.

22

Reaching the trees, walk along the right hand side. Ignore the first gap in the hedge on the left with a footpath marker but go through the gap a few yards further along. Keep to the right hand boundary over stiles to reach the road by the church.

A little way down the lane to the right is the Golden Lion. The route of the walk, however, is to the left. It is worth looking into the churchyard opposite for over the wall you will see ancient Luddesdowne Court, claimed to be the longest continuously occupied dwelling in the country. Continuing the walk, keep the church on the right as you follow the waymarked path towards a farm complex. On the left you will find a stile with the letters 'WW' on it. This means you are on another of Kent's long distance paths, the Weald Way, which runs from Gravesend to the Sussex coast.

Over the stile, follow the left boundary of the field towards rising ground. In the top left corner look for a Weald Way signpost for Great Buckland. Keep to the trees along the ridge. On the left is a valley known as Bowling Alley. Cross a stile into the next field and go diagonally left for a stile a short distance away. Follow a well-used path diagonally right across several fields to a stile and then up some steps to join a narrow lane.

A right turn takes you soon to a fork where you go up the left, no-through road. You pass several houses in extensive grounds. Look out on the right for the little church of Dode. Continue up the tree-lined lane until you reach an obvious gas-pipe installation.

Immediately before it, take a signposted byway. The track rises steeply and at the top turn right to rejoin the North Downs Way. Soon you reach the car park.

Luddesdowne - Historical Notes

Luddesdowne: The sheltered valleys in the area encouraged early man to settle here. There is evidence of farming taking place as far back as 2000 BC. In Saxon times it was owned by Lewin, brother of King Harold. On Lewin's death at the Battle of Hastings, it came into the possession of the Norman Bishop Odo of Bayeux.

Luddesdowne Court: Claimed to be the longest continuously lived-in building in the land, the house can still show work of Saxon and Norman builders. It is believed it was built on the site of an Iron Age hut. Features of the house are a Norman dovecote, a Tudor chimney and a gallery. In the Great Hall one can still see drawings of ships scratched in the plaster possibly in the fourteenth century. It is not open to the public.

Luddesdowne Church: The oldest part of the present building dates back to the thirteenth century. Among the unusual relics of the church of St Peter and St Paul are a stone coffin lid of about the same period and a thirteenth century staircase leading to the belfry made from roughly hewn tree trunks and logs. The church has three ancient bells, the oldest being early fifteenth century.

Dode Church: The peaceful Norman church of Dode gives no hint today that it was once the centre of a thriving village wiped out in the Bubonic Plague, or Black Death, which swept England in 1348–9. The Plague was brought to England from the East and the numerous rats and their fleas which infested most towns and villages proved ideal carriers of the disease. This was, and is, highly contagious and it spread rapidly from London. Some estimates place

24

the proportion of the population that died from this first epidemic as high as a third. Communities withered, no food was produced and villages such as Dode were simply abandoned.

The church was later united with the neighbouring church of Paddlesworth. It was originally thatched but a roof of tiles was put on when the building was restored in 1905 by a Gravesend worthy, George Arnold and his wife, Elizabeth. When the Roman Catholics re-opened the church for a major service after World War II, the point was made that no Protestant service had ever been held there.

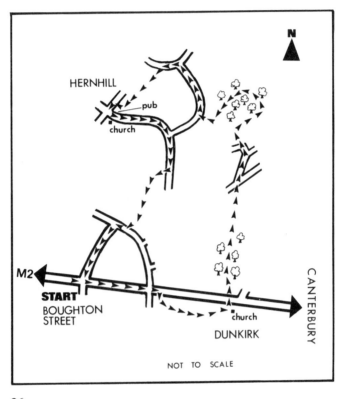

Boughton-under-Blean and Hernhill

Introduction: The particular pleasure of this walk is that you are several times given superb, almost aerial, views of the widening Thames Estuary, Whitstable and the Isle of Sheppey, as you are on high ground for much of the time. The area is within Kent's major fruit-growing region so there are orchards to contrast with the woodland on the high ground, full of history because it was there that Mad Thom, a revolutionary figure of the early nineteenth century, had his base. The walk begins at Boughton-under-Blean, also known as Boughton Street. The main street through it, which once bore the burden of all the main traffic to Canterbury and Dover is now by-passed and is a delightful backwater. It is possible now to enjoy in peace the village architecture which spans several centuries.

Distance: The route is about 5 miles long taking a leisurely 2½ hours.

Refreshments: Boughton-under-Blean has a number of pubs which serve food and about two-thirds of the way round is the village of Hernhill, where the Red Lion pub provides snacks.

How to get there: Boughton-under-Blean is by-passed by the A2 trunk road between Faversham and Canterbury. The road to the village is a very short distance from Brenley Corner at the end of the M2 motorway.

The Walk: Go along the village street towards Canterbury. Part of the way is by delightful period houses; the pavements are on banks above the roadway. On the outskirts, go up an alley on the right just beyond the 40mph sign.

Where the footway begins to veer right go up a path between mesh fending and a row of houses on the right. At a road, walk ahead through modern houses to a junction and take the no-through road - Dunkirk Road. At another junction go up the rough track ahead.

The path narrows before you reach a gate into a vast area of gorse-covered heath, rising high in front of you. Follow a path ahead on the rising ground and soon behind you, you will have your first fine view of the Thames Estuary and the Swale - the channel between the Isle of Sheppey and the mainland.

There are a number of paths here going in various directions, but if you look ahead you will see a line of windbreak trees on the brow of the hill. Make for the left-hand end of the trees. A few yards from them you will see a stile. Cross it, go forward for a few yards and then bear left to another stile near a house. Join a narrow path running between the gardens of private houses. Soon you emerge at a lane serving Dunkirk Church, with its square flinty tower.

A left turn takes you to a main road where you cross over towards the drive of a large building opposite. At the entrance to the drive, take the rough path to the left. Where it veers right, go ahead through a gate to pass a cottage on the right.

Follow the path through the trees to a road junction with another Thames vista to the left.

A private road (bridleway) opposite leads you to a fork

where you go left. The driveway turns into a house on the left, but you continue forward on a narrow woodland path where it can be sometimes muddy underfoot after rain. The track makes a huge U-turn and on the further bend, the panorama of the Thames Estuary as it widens by Whistable opens up. The fern-lined path begins to descend and follows a fence on the right to a lane.

Go right to a T-junction and then take the left-hand road. After an open field on the left, look out for steps in the left bank to a stile marked by a signpost. Follow the line of fruit trees in the orchard to a stile by a row of houses. Emerge at the road and bear left to reach the centre of Hernhill and the Red Lion pub. Take the lane to the left in front of the pub - Crockham Lane - with orchards on either side. At a road junction go right. Pass a drive to a house on the left.

Where a very tall hedge on the right gives way to a much lower hedge, go up the track on the right. Halfway between the road and a field gate you will find a stile on the left. A brief climb up a sloping pasture brings you to a stile into an orchard. Strictly, the right of way goes through the middle of the trees, but you will find it simpler to walk round the outside edge to the right. Keep on the boundary path and make for a tall windbreak of trees. Walk alongside the trees, keeping them on your right. Drop down the slope towards a house, veer left before the road and walk along the edge of the orchard for a few yards until you see a gap in the right-hand boundary. Exit to the road. A few yards to the right take the lane between hall hedges to the left. This will take you back to the centre of Boughton-under-Blean.

Boughton-under-Blean - Historical Notes

Boughton-under-Blean Church: The thirteenth century church of St Peter and St Paul has a fifteenth century tower.

Its main interest is a monument by the seventeenth century English sculptor Epiphanius Evesham. It shows the armoured figure of Sir Thomas Hawkins and his wife, Anne. Carved panels on the side show their seven sons and six daughters, one a girl with a handkerchief to her eyes and a boy holding a ball. Also buried in the church was another Hawkins who lived to be 101 - very rare in those days.

Hernhill: The place where Mad Thom was buried in the parish churchyard is not known. Sad, because he was one of Kent's most colourful personalities. In the 1830s he came to Kent from Cornwall and wearing dress as flamboyant as his manner described himself at various times as Sir William Courtenay, Knight of Malta, Baron Rothschild and the King of Jerusalem. He was so plausible that after a spell in Maidstone Gaol, he stood for Parliament for Canterbury and polled 450 votes although he was not elected. John Nicholls Thom (his real name) lived in Hernhill after a stay in a mental asylum. In 1838 he headed discontented farm workers, who thought of him as a Messiah, in an uprising against authority. Soldiers were sent to Blean Wood near Canterbury where he and eight of his followers were killed in a skirmish.

Dunkirk Church: One of the better results of the lawlessness in the area led by Thom was the building of Christ Church in 1840. It is said that flints from the old Canterbury city walls were used in its construction.

Leigh and Penshurst Place

Introduction: Some of the finest areas in which to walk today are near great estates in which the wealthy lived. When the great families of the past built their country homes, they not unnaturally chose sites where the rural scenery was at its best. In this walk you circumnavigate a splendid stately home, once the home of Henry VIII and the celebrated Elizabethan courtier-poet Philip Sidney. You also walk along the bank of the river Medway, at this point quite narrow and edged with a great variety of wild flowers.

Distance: The walk is about 6 to 7 miles long and should take about 3 hours.

Refreshments: In the villages of Leigh and Penshurst there are public houses which serve food. Penshurst has at least two places where you may find afternoon tea.

How to get there: Leigh, the starting point is best reached on the B2027 from Hildenborough on the B245 London to Tonbridge road. There is plenty of parking space, particularly near Leigh village green.

The walk: Leave the green by Green View Avenue alongside the sports pavilion. If you are lucky you may see a

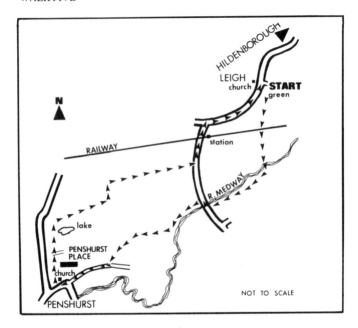

game of stoolball, an ancestor of cricket, on the green, as there is a local side.

At the end of the residential road, a stile takes you down a wooded track under a railway bridge. Walk between mesh fences to a stile and then follow the right boundary of a pasture through a one-time gate across another pasture to an easily seen metal footbridge over the river.

The path goes left briefly and over a small bridge over a stream. Go ahead for a short distance to a squeeze stile. About 20 yards to the right you will find a stile and plank over a ditch into a large field. The route here is part of the Eden Valley Walk. Follow the right boundary as far as you can to a stile by a gate leading to a road.

Walk right, over a bridge and take the stile on the left immediately on the other side. Follow the bank of the Medway ahead. About 250 yards along when you see a house with red hanging tiles on rising ground to the right, walk away from the river bank to find a metal bridge over a ditch.

Climb up the grass slope beside a line of marker posts towards the right side of the house at the top. A stile by a gate takes you on a concrete farm road going in about the same direction. Where the hard road bears left, go straight ahead on a rough track towards trees.

Beyond them go diagonally left downhill to the farthest corner. On the way look ahead to pick out the roofs and towers of Penshurst Place. A stile in the corner leads to another stile; beyond it you join a road to Penshurst Place and the village.

Go through the arch to the main road and then bear right, crossing the quaint courtyard and under the arch formed by living quarters above to the church. A footpath on the left round the side leads to the park of Penshurst Place. Walk ahead over the grass, parallel with the great house on the right. Continue ahead to a squeeze stile to the right of some double gates. Cross a drive and stride out towards another squeeze stile in the distant boundary fence, following a wide grassy ride between the trees. You will notice a cricket pitch on the right.

Keep parallel with a line of very tall trees on the left. A lake can be seen beyond the fence on the right. Cross the stile and follow the boundary to the right. At another stile go left up a slight slope on a grass area between an avenue of splendid trees. After a stile, the path goes uphill through a woodland walk with abundant wild flowers. At the top of the slope go right to join an avenue of fine trees. Look out on the right for views of the country through gaps in the trees. Walk ahead up the avenue after a stile and where the lines of trees end, go forward in the same direction. There is a fine view across the countryside on the left with the line of the greensand ridge beyond.

The path goes through trees to a stile by a metal gate and ends at a public lane where you go left passing Leigh station. At the T-junction, a right turn takes you back to the green at the village.

Leigh and Penshurst Place — Historical Notes

Penshurst Place: The focal point of the great house is the wonderful medieval Great Hall built by Sir John de Pulteney about 1340 which is virtually unchanged to this day. The building was greatly added to during the reign of Queen Elizabeth I. It became the home of the Sidney family in 1552. The most famous member perhaps was Sir Philip Sidney, a favourite of Queen Elizabeth I. He was a poet and his verses entitled *Arcadia* were supposed to have been inspired by the rural scene round Penshurst. In 1586 he was wounded in battle at Zutphen in the Low Countries during the war against Spain and when offered water, he refused and asked for it to be given to a soldier, with the immortal words: 'Thy necessity is greater than mine.' His wound became gangrenous and he died soon afterwards.

Penshurst Place is open every afternoon (except Mondays) from April 1st, until the first Sunday in October. It is open on Bank Holiday Mondays and Good Friday.

Penshurst Church: It is outstanding because of its Perpendicular tower with pinnacles at each corner. Most of the body of the building was built in the twelfth and thirteenth centuries, but there were many alterations made in the nineteenth century. The main memorials are in the Sidney

Chapel. One is the thirteenth century figure of Sir Stephen de Penchester and the tomb of Sir William Sidney, the first of the family to live at Penshurst.

Leigh Parish Church: St Mary's at Leigh (pronounced Lie) stands on the highest ground in the village and overlooks the green. Its medieval structure underwent considerable changes in 1860-1. It has a fifteenth century font, a seventeenth century pulpit and a window in the north wall depicting the Virgin and Child dates from the fourteenth century. A wrought iron hour glass stand dated 1597 is to be found on the pulpit.

Stoolball: Played in a number of villages in south-west Kent and East Sussex, stoolball is a forerunner of cricket. The wickets, 16 yards apart, are a board a foot square on a pole 4 feet 8 inches high. The bat is rather like an oversized table tennis bat and the ball is made of rubber. There are eight balls to the over.

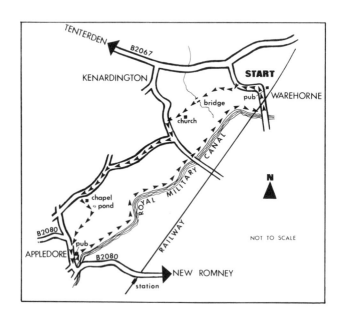

The Royal
Military Canal

Introduction: The first half of this walk goes through pleasant farmland with the second leg along three miles of the Canal, owned by the National Trust. The Royal Military Canal was built in Napoleonic times for defence along what had been the coastline in Saxon times, when most of the Romney Marsh was under water.

Distance: This six mile walk is one of the most easy-going possible, and can be done in 2½ to 3 hours at a leisurely pace.

Refreshments: There is the Woolpack Inn at Warehorne, but more opportunity for food can be found at Appledore at the other end of the circuit.

How to get there: My preference is to start the walk at Warehorne, but it could just as easily be at Appledore. In any case make by road to Tenterden, and for Warehorne take the B2067 via Woodchurch, and Kenardington. For Appledore, drive on the B2080 from Tenterden.

The walk: Having parked in Warehorne, walk back along the road keeping the church on the left. As the road begins to curve right, take the farm road on the left opposite a concrete track. But only briefly, for you have to use the gate a few yards along on the right. Walk across the middle of the field to a stile in the hedge. Continue downhill in the middle of the next field to cross a ditch with a stile.

Immediately on the left is a gate leading to a field with a few fruit trees in it. Cross diagonally towards the right hand corner. Just before the corner take the stile on the right. Walk left and find another gate a few yards from the corner.

Bear slightly right to reach a metal footbridge over a watercourse, then a plank over a ditch. Veer right to several stiles and make your way to Kenardington churchyard, on the way looking out over the marshes to the left. It was in these fields by the churchyard that King Alfred built earthworks as a defence against the Danes.

From the churchyard follow a drive to the junction. Then turn left and go down a pleasant quiet lane to a T-junction where you go right. At a main road walk left. After you pass the entrance to Gusbourne Farm on the left, look out, a few yards further along, for another farm entrance with a footpath signpost. A few yards along on the left is Hornes Place which has a medieval chapel which may be visited by appointment on Wednesdays between 10am and 5pm.

Continue through several field gates with a large pond on the left and a hedge on the right. At the end of the pond, go left along the bottom end to a wire fence. Do not use the stile there, but walk along the fence to the right. You are in a long, narrow pasture. Go right to the end for a stile and plank bridge in the right hand corner. In the adjacent field follow a ditch on the left until you reach a stile on the left. Ignore it and turn right to reach the recreation ground at Appledore. At the main road turn left to go through the village.

A few yards past the Red Lion on the left, go into the National Trust property which runs alongside the Royal Military Canal. The whole area is grassed over with plenty of trees. In places you have a choice of walking along the higher ground with views over the marshes, or you can follow the more sheltered ground on the left.

When you reach a farm on the left, cross over the narrow lane and continue on the slightly wilder bank of the canal ahead. The way takes you under a railway bridge and a little further on, to a lane. Here you leave the footpath and take the road to the left back to Warehorne.

The Royal Military Canal - Historical Notes

Warehorne: The thirteenth century church of St Matthew has several windows hundreds of years old and pillars of marble. The lords of the manor traditionally held their courts at the ancient Woolpack Inn, to which local people came to pay their dues. These ceased about 50 years ago and the occasion was marked by the then lady of the manor by the gift to the village of the green.

Kenardington Church: The tower of St Mary's Church built in the twelfth century, is the oldest part of the church which was burned by the French in the fourteenth century and set on fire again in 1559 when struck by lightning. The church was repaired using much of the old material. The belfry is reached by an unusual outside circular staircase.

Appledore: When the sea was near the village, the place was a ship-building centre and the wide main street has the feel of a traditional prosperity. The parish had its stirring times. The Danes built a fort on the site of the present parish church of St Peter and St Paul when they occupied the village. Six hundred years ago, the church was burned when the French pillaged the area.

The Royal Military Canal: The waterway between Hythe in Kent and Rye in Sussex was built by Prime Minister Pitt between 1804 and 1809. It was primarily a defence work against a possible invasion by Napoleon across the vulnerable Romney Marsh, but Pitt persuaded local landowners to co-operate by assuring them that it would be useful as a means of local transport and marsh drainage. The eminent engineer, John Rennie supervised the work. The invasion never came and it was never used for transport. It was fortified with pill boxes during World War II and some may still be seen.

The White Cliffs of Dover

Introduction: England has no better and more charismatic physical feature than the White Cliffs of Dover. About half this walk is along the top of them with the French coast visible across the Channel on many days of the year. Efforts are being made to preserve the best of the British coastline of which this stretch is a prime example and farmland edging the cliff top is now owned by the National Trust. The area is rich in wild flowers and butterflies, and by turning the head in the other direction you have the panorama of the busiest shipping lane in the world.

Distance: This 5½ mile walk will take about 2½ hours at a leisurely pace.

Refreshments: The Coastguard pub is near the beach parking area where the walk starts and ends. At Kingsdown, the half way mark, the Zetland Arms is also right on the shingle sand beach with the Rising Sun a few yards inland.

How to get there: At the roundabout on the A2 on the outskirts of Dover, take the left hand turning marked to Deal. A short distance along, look for the road to the right signposted St Margaret's. At a T-junction go right into the village of St Margaret's at Cliffe and carry on down the road, steep and

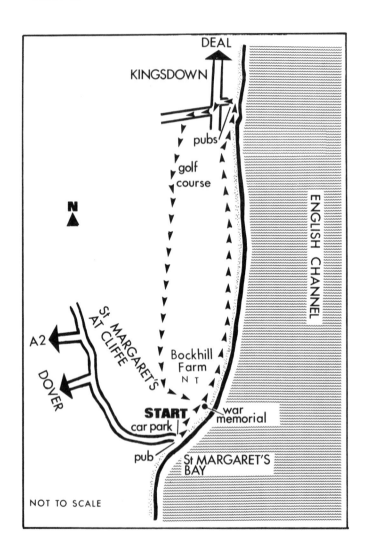

with sharp bends in places, to St Margaret's Bay, where you have parking a few yards from the sea.

The walk: After parking, find the steps going up the cliff-side just beyond the public toilets. At the top take the path to the right, go right at the fork and then right at the National Trust sign for The Leas.

As you walk through the area of grass and wild flowers you have the Channel on the right and on the left houses on a bank with an enviable view from their front windows. Looking back you will see the South Foreland lighthouse on the cliff top beyond St Margaret's Bay. Soon ahead of you, you will see the needle-like obelisk of the Dover Patrol Memorial. Pass the obelisk and continue along the grassy clifftop path with the cliffs a short distance to the right.

As the sea birds swoop near you, look ahead to enjoy the view up the Kent coast as far as the North Foreland jutting out beyond the waters of Pegwell Bay. Just inland are the giant cooling towers of Richborough Power Station. The way goes pleasantly along the undulating cliff edge. If you have children or a dog with you watch out for the dangers in that direction.

Presently you will see a golf course on the left and ahead the coastal village of Kingsdown. The path begins to go downhill to some steps to the road by the now disused firing range. Walk along Undercliffe Road until the fencing ends and you can get on to the beach if you can cope with the slithery, sliding shingle.

The Zetland Arms is on the beach end of a row of buildings ahead. Beyond the pub go up the picturesque little street to the road again. Follow it round to the left as it goes uphill through the village street.

Coming out of the village at the other end, look for a footpath between houses which is marked with a sign stone on the left opposite St James' Road. You walk through trees and at an intersection of paths go right, to the road. Kingsdown International Scout Campsite is on the left.

Walk down the road to the right and at a T-junction go right. At a major road walk right. A few yards down on the left you will find a bridleway marked by a stone. For a while you follow wooden garden fences to a fork where you go left by a row of conifers. Cross over and take the clear path across an open field with views of the sea over to the left. Follow the path alongside a thick hedge on the left. Eventually the route becomes enclosed by woodland. At an open field cross it almost to the far left corner where a gap by a white post leads you out to a track. Go right along this between hedges and on rising ground. At the top of the rise, you will see a hedge coming in obliquely towards the path from the left. Leave the main track and follow this hedge on a narrow path to the left so that, in effect, you wil be going back slightly in direction.

At the National Trust sign for Bockhill Farm follow the easily found path as it bends round to the right and crosses open downland towards the obelisk war memorial. When the track eventually bears right go straight on along the field edge, following a waymarked path. With the obelisk on your right begin to veer over to the right and retrace your steps down the steepish slope into the trees and back down the steps into St Margaret's Bay.

The White Cliffs of Dover — Historical Notes

St Margaret's Bay: The creeper-covered white cliffs provide a sheltered sun-trap for the shingle beach. It is so mild that although the sea was only a few yards away, roses grew well in the gardens of a row of picturesque cottages at the cliff base. The houses were smashed when the Germans bombarded the coast from artillery on the French side of the Channel in World War II.

Dover Patrol Memorial: The obelisk was set up in memory of the men of the Dover Patrol who died on active service in World War I and was continued as a memorial to the men of the Royal Navy and the Merchant Service who were killed in the Dover Strait in World War II. The foundation stone was laid by Prince Arthur of Connaught in November 1919 and the memorial was unveiled by the Prince of Wales in July 1927. There are similar memorials at Cap Blanc Nez in France and New York Harbour.

Bockhill Farm: The farm and the walk along the cliff edge was bought by the National Trust in 1974 as part of its Enterprise Neptune campaign which aimed at acquiring and preserving areas of unspoilt coastline. Parish councils in the neighbourhood contributed other land. The area is rich in bird life including the fulmar and the kittiwake.

St Margaret's-at-Cliffe: The parish has one of the finest Norman churches in the country, St Margaret's being practically unaltered since it was built. Smugglers were said to have stored ropes and other tackle in the belfry. They used to haul contraband up the cliff face from the beach.

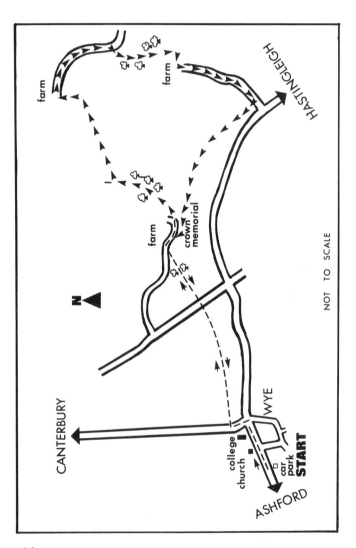

N

NOT TO SCALE

CANTERBURY

HASTINGLEIGH

WYE

ASHFORD

START

college
church
car
park

crown
memorial

farm

farm

farm

farm

Wye and
The North Downs Way

Introduction: This walk runs for quite a distance along the top of the North Downs with stunning views over the Ashford area. There is a nature reserve nearby, but the whole district is blessed with plentiful wild flowers and butterflies. Wye itself has a youthful population for much of the year at Wye Agricultural College, part of London University. A landmark to look for is a large crown cut in the chalk of the hillside nearby.

Distance: The walk is about 5 miles long with good going underfoot and will take about 2½ hours.

Refreshments: Wye itself has several good pubs and cafes catering for the inner man or woman, but there are no places for refreshment along the way.

How to get there: Wye can best be reached by turning off the A28 Ashford to Canterbury road about five miles north of Ashford. There is a free car park in the centre of Wye.

The walk: Aim for the church and walk in front of it in an easterly direction. You immediately pass Wye College, part of London University, and the coat of arms at the entrance, showing three stooks of corn, gives notice that the speciality there is agriculture. Go round the corner by the garden with a fountain playing into Olantigh Road.

Just before the last college building on the left, go up the hard road through College farmland and buildings called Occupation Road on the right. You will see experimental plantations, greenhouses and a clutch of weather recording instruments as you walk on. The road becomes rougher between tall trees and eventually reaches a lane. On the way look half right to see the crown etched in the chalk of the downs. Cross over the road into the field opposite and follow the clear path ahead slightly uphill to woodland. Note the black, blue and white acorn sign which indicates that you are on a long distance path, the North Downs Way.

A gate takes you into the trees and between fences. At the top of the rise continue ahead to a lane. Walk right here. It is worth a short pause to admire the splendid view of sharply sloping downland and the fine trees to the left. The lane runs uphill and at the top where the built-up road goes left to serve a farm, you go straight on using a stile by a metal gate. Follow the tall hedge on the left, pass a wooden gate at the end and then continue for about 75 yards. Go through a gate and then follow the path round to the left and along the woodland edge with trees on the right and an open field on the left.

At an obvious point where the copse on your right ends and the line of trees thins out, go right into an open field. The right of way is half left down the hill to a gate on the further side. If there is no clear way through standing crops, you will be able to walk round the field to the left. The track beyond the gate goes left to another gate which you do not use. Instead walk downhill against the field boundary with the fence on your left. There are magnificent views of this fold in the top of the downs on either side.

Reaching a concrete farm road go left and just before

48

some green water tanks, take the made-up road to the right. Pass a house and garden on the right and go down the narrow path running downhill among trees. At the concrete farm road ahead go right through farm buildings and a gate to a wide track. Several hundred feet along this, at a point where the trees on either side of the path meet overhead, take a bridleway going off into the trees on the right.

Emerging into a field keep in the same direction following a left boundary to a gate. Walk ahead between fences for about 20 yards to an iron gate. There go right following the fence slightly downhill. At a concrete farm road go left. Notice the handsome modern farm buildings. The road goes uphill for quite a while with plenty of wild flowers on the grassy bank.

Just before the gate to the road, go through a field gate on the right marked North Downs Way. After another gate a short distance ahead, follow the right hand fence along the ridge of the downs with the marvellous view to the left. After a stile go ahead towards trees and stay on the ridge. The fence on the right leads you to a stile in the corner. Follow the path over a stile to another stile to a lane - which you came up earlier - and turn left.

About 100 yards on the left leave the road following the North Downs Way. To remind you, you go through the wood to a gate. Then cross a field to a lane which you cross to enter the college land and back to Wye.

Wye - Historical Notes

Wye Church: The church was built by Cardinal Kempe, a friend of Henry V and a native of Wye. In 1572 lightning set the church alight and a century later, the tower collapsed causing considerable damage. A new tower was built in a different part of the church.

Wye: Two women of interest were born here. Mrs Aphra Behn, the local barber's daughter, was sent on an espionage mission to Antwerp by Charles II, and was thought to be England's first woman novelist. She was buried in Westminster Abbey. The other was Catherine Macaulay, known to Dr Johnson in his day. Legend has it that she was banned from the Reading Room of the British Museum after she tore some pages from a manuscript.

Wye Nature Reserve: On the outskirts of Wye is a nature reserve of uncultivated downland and woodland preserved by the Nature Conservancy Council. The huge depression in the hillside is known as the Devil's Kneadingtrough.

Shoreham and Otford

Introduction: Shoreham is in the valley of the river Darent which rises in Westerham and empties into the Thames at Dartford. This walk runs briefly alongside the Darent as it goes through the village and then climbs the hillside on the east side to remote farmland on the other side giving magnificent views across the valley. The return is on part of the North Downs Way and via the village of Otford. The fertility and sheltered position of the Darent Valley encouraged a wealthy Roman to build a villa at Lullingstone; the Normans to build a castle at Eynsford. More recently, the world renowned artist, the late Graham Sutherland spent his early married life in the valley and earlier another famous painter, Samuel Palmer, lived and worked in Shoreham.

Distance: This 7 mile ramble will take about 3½ hours.

Refreshments: Shoreham and Otford are well provided in this respect and half way round the walk there is the Fox and Hounds in the hamlet of Romney Street which serves a good range of hot and cold food.

How to get there: Shoreham Station is on the A225 between Otford and Farningham and can therefore be reached

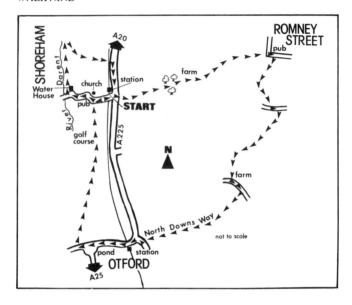

conveniently from the A25 and the A20. There is parking in the forecourt of the station.

The walk: Having parked in the station forecourt, take the steps down to the road and bear right for Shoreham. Not far down the tree-lined lane you will see on the green hill on the other side of the valley, the huge cross carved out of the grass - the local war memorial.

Passing the entrance to Darenth Valley Golf Club and Shoreham Place, you will soon reach that typical English village grouping of pub – the Old George Inne – and the parish church with its avenue of cypress trees leading to the porch.

Further down the road, the rushing of water indicates a small cascade and stream which runs into the Darent. An old parapet bridge crosses the river, but you do not go over it. Instead walk to the right towards a large white house in its own enclosed garden. This is Water House, the home of the 19th century artist Samuel Palmer. Walk to the left of it alongside the little river. You have another good view of the memorial cross on the hillside on the left. When the waterside path reaches a row of cottages with gardens paddling in the water, take a path to the right by a footbridge and then a stile to follow a well-defined path on raised ground through a field.

You cross a stream through a tunnel of trees and pass a white house on the right. A stile takes you across an open field to the railway line which you must cross with care. Through a little gate on the other side you reach the main road.

Walk along the road to the right to Shoreham Station. Opposite it is Copt Hall and you take the track uphill through trees on the further side of it. At a fork keep left. There follows a severe climb but it does not last too long. Go forward at a cross track at the top and go across a field to the left of a green corrugated iron farm building. Walk through the middle of the farmyard to a farm track going slightly downhill on the other side. You are in a pleasant little valley.

Go down the slope, up the other side and then pass through a gap in the field boundary on the left to walk diagonally across several fields to a stile among trees.

The small woodland leads to a stile overlooking a splendid valley. Go ahead slightly left down the grassy slope dotted with small trees to find a stile on the floor of the valley. Go ahead over a grass path between the fairways of a golf course. Coming to a stile, go into a field on the right, and climb up the steel slope following the left hand boundary.

Where trees end on the left, continue straight ahead uphill and at the top climb over two stiles in quick succession into a field. Continue ahead down a slope and reaching trees on the right, go ahead uphill towards the brow. Pass some trees on the right and ahead you will see a chimney and roof which is your aim. At a stile go through a paddock and down a fenced alley to the road where you will find the Fox and Hounds.

Leaving the pub take the stile immediately opposite and cross the large pasture ahead to the bottom right hand corner, where you will find a gap in the boundary. Walk left down the narrow pasture bounded by trees on either side to a stile at the end. Stay with the right boundary to a stile for a little path to a lane. Here walk left briefly. At the end of a garden on the right go over a stile into a field. Walk right, keeping the handsome garden already mentioned on the right initially. When the fence begins to curve away to the right continue straight on along a vague, grassy path towards a line of trees. In the next boundary, under some trees, drop down steeply into a lovely little valley and up the other side to a stile. The path runs through woodland for some time and then alongside fences to reach a lane. Turn left by The Granary and Paines Farm and walk along the lane for about 150 yards or so to find a stile in the hedge on the right. Eventually, the enclosed path opens up into a field and there is an easily seen track into woodland where you will find a stile with a black and yellow symbol indicating that you have now joined the North Downs Way.

There is a magnificent view across the Darent valley as you follow the track downhill to a road. There you go right and soon join the main road through the valley. There go left following the North Downs Way markers. Pass Otford station on the left into the village centre and go on the road ahead with the pond and its picturesque weeping willows on the left. Immediately past a garden shop on the right go up a farm road with a signpost to Shoreham. Soon you have the hills of the valley on either side. Where the farm road bears to the left you continue forward on a narrow path. Follow the path to a stile and then along a lengthy, fenced path between the fairways of a golf course. Cross a track and continue along the path to the road. Turn right for the railway station.

Shoreham and Otford - Historical Notes

Shoreham Church: The church has one of the finest porches in the country, dating from the 15th century. The entrance is formed from the root of a huge upended oak. On the west wall is a painting showing the scene over 100 years ago when the son of the vicar, Lieutenant Verney Cameron RN was welcomed by the villagers on his return from Africa after he made the first east to west crossing of the continent. The Dean and Chapter of Westminster Abbey nominate the vicars of Shoreham. Presumably as a result of this, the church has an organ case and pulpit which were originally in the Abbey. In the south wall is a window created by the artist Burne-Jones dedicated to Sir Joseph Prestwich, a Victorian geologist.

Water House: Samuel Palmer, the Victorian artist lived there with his father and old nurse from 1827 to 1833. His friend and mentor the poet and painter, William Blake visited Palmer at Water House.

Otford: Otford made its mark early in history because of its strategic position on the Pilgrims' Way with the crossing of the river Darent at that point. One of the many palaces of the Archbishops of Canterbury was built there. Thomas Becket was said to have smote the ground with his staff in the manner of Moses to bring forth a water supply for the palace, and to have stopped birds from singing in the grounds. The last of the palaces was a sumptuous one rivalling Hampton Court, built by Archbishop Warham in the sixteenth century, and a companion to the great house of Knole near Sevenoaks. King Henry VIII stayed at Otford with 4,000 followers on his way to the Field of the Cloth of Gold meeting with the King of France in 1520.

Leeds and Leeds Castle

Introduction: Leeds Castle, sitting on two small islands in a lake, has been rightly described as the most beautiful castle in the world. How fortunate it is for the Kent rambler that because public rights of way run through the grounds, it is possible to incorporate a close view of it in the course of a walk! One is able to inject a sense of drama by setting off in the village of Leeds - itself full of history and charm - and first of all obtaining a fine distant view of the castle amid the trees before the climax of walking right alongside the lake round the historic building. As with so many rambles in North Kent, the long line of the Downs forms a backdrop to the scenery.

Distance: The walk of 5 miles is for the most part over fairly even ground and will take about 2½ hours.

Refreshments: There are several pubs which provide food in the village.

How to get there: Leeds village is about a mile south of the M20, 7 miles east of Maidstone. It is well signposted because the castle attracts thousands of visitors. The village is a short distance beyond the main entrance to the castle grounds. There is a public car park alongside the parish

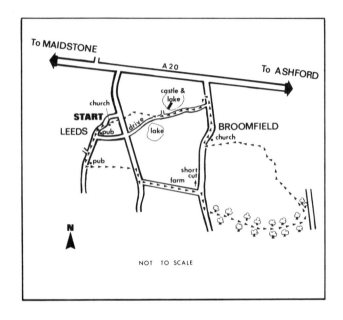

To MAIDSTONE

A 20

To ASHFORD

castle & lake

church

START

LEEDS

pub

drive

lake

BROOMFIELD

church

pub

short cut

farm

N

NOT TO SCALE

church, which with its unusually wide tower and somewhat incongruously small steeple, is easily found.

The walk: Walk left from the car park through the long straggling village. Pass several white weather boarded and red brick houses and the George Inn. Just past the junction on the left, note the black and white timber framed Manor House with ancient stone windows.

It is all that remains of a large Wealden house. The land behind it was the site of a twelfth century abbey. Beyond, the pavement runs on a higher level than the road for a while. Look out for a half-timbered house called Vineys and the

58

Ten Bells pub on the left. About 50 yards beyond the police house go through a wide gap in the hedge and follow the left boundary of the field and then a line of poles to a lane. There are good views of the North Downs.

At the lane, go right for a few yards to take the lane to the left. On this stretch of the walk look for your first sight of Leeds Castle. Pass a farm followed by a line of conifers. At a T-junction at the end of the lane, go right. (At this point should you want to shorten the walk, go left down the lane past Broomfield Church and further on past an entrance to Leeds Castle).

Taking the longer route, continue down the lane to the south and at the bottom of a dip in the road go left on a marked footpath through woodland. Ignore all side paths until you reach a stile. Take the main path which bears slightly half left through more trees. Look out for a track through the woods to the left a short distance before you reach a lane. The path veers slightly to the left. Keep a sharp eye on the right side for a point where a field starts. Go through the narrow fringe of trees to the fence to find a stile into a field.

Walk obliquely left across the field northwards towards the trees in the next boundary. Bear right to the corner of the woodland and then veer diagonally left to the far corner of a large field where there is a stile. Walk ahead towards the red-roofed Broomfield church. Cross a stile into the churchyard.

Walk through the churchyard to the lane and go right, until you reach an entrance to Leeds Castle grounds where there is a golf course. As the public right of way does not go through the gateway you have to walk about 100 paces to a little gate in a mesh fence on the left. Once you are inside the grounds of Leeds Castle, it is essential that you stay strictly on the route described here. This is a public right of way and you are entitled to walk it. But if you leave it you may be challenged by the staff of the castle and asked to pay the admission price to the grounds.

Walk down the slight slope and then left keeping the golfing green on your right. Walk through trees to the right of a jutting box hedge to the driveway through the park. Walk right on this and very soon you will be walking by the lake forming the moat round the castle and the entrancing building itself. Follow the drive as it veers round to the right between two lakes to the main entrance to the castle over a small arched bridge. Here, take the drive to the left noting the grey ruins, one of the oldest parts of the castle, on the right.

Ignore the driveway marked 'way out' going to the right, but continue ahead on the driveway with the lake on the left. You will see a footpath stone at this point. Reaching a cattle grid, leave the drive.

Walk across the grass half right towards a series of marker posts to the right the driveway further up. You should find no difficulty as the grass is more trimly cut. Continue half right up a grass slope to another marker post and further on to a yellow topped post by the entrance to a cricket ground. Keep to the right boundary to another gate into a small pasture. Straight ahead is a gate to a lane. Cross over, noting grey-stoned Battell Hall on the left, for another gate which takes you straight ahead to Leeds Church and the car park.

Leeds - Historical Notes

Leeds: The village which straggles up a rising street, figures in the Domesday Book. One of Kent's vineyards was there. Nothing substantial remains of the Augustinian priory founded in Leeds in 1119 which became one of the wealthiest monasteries in the land. Among interesting buildings in the village are Battell Hall, near the church, a restored fifteenth century house, and a half-timbered group of dwellings known as Vineys in the main street.

Leeds Church: St Nicholas' Church has a Norman tower of such square and substantial proportions that it is thought it might have been built in the first place as a form of defence. In the churchyard is the grave of James Barham, who in 1761, helped ring 40,320 Bob Majors in 27 hours at the church. He died in 1818 aged 93. In 1878, a series of jars of thirteenth century pottery were found in the walls. They were apparently put there to help the acoustics of the church. Prominent in the church is a Victorian coat of arms which once stood over the entrance to a furniture shop in Dover.

Broomfield: The parish was the home of the Hatch family of bell-makers. Joseph made 150 bells for Kent belfries. One of the bells in Broomfield Church dated 1663 has inscribed on it: 'William Hatch made me'.

Leeds Castle: Standing on two islands on a lake in a park designed by Capability Brown, this ancient grey building has been described many times as the most beautiful castle in the world. Today it is known to thousands for it has become part of the tourist industry in a big way. But not so many years ago, its attractions were rarely seen by the public who could only penetrate the woodlands masking it from the main road by a few footpaths. The castle was bought by Lady Baillie in 1926 and after her death, a charitable trust was set up in 1974 to preserve it as a centre for medical research, the arts and charity work. The original castle was built by Robert de Crevecoeur in the twelfth century and part of the present building goes back to the thirteenth and fourteenth centuries. It was owned by royalty for three hundred years; eight Queens lived there. Still standing is the gatehouse built by Edward I who regarded Leeds as his favourite castle. Much rebuilding was done in the nineteenth century harmonising with the older parts. In the fourteenth and fifteenth centuries the castle was used as a prison. The seventeenth century diarist John Evelyn was in charge of 500 French and Dutch prisoners kept there. One previous owner was Thomas Fairfax, a stalwart for Cromwell's cause and a general in the Parliamentary army, who played a crucial role in the Battle of Maidstone when the King's men were routed from the county town.